ANIMALS, NATURE
and
ALBERT SCHWEITZER

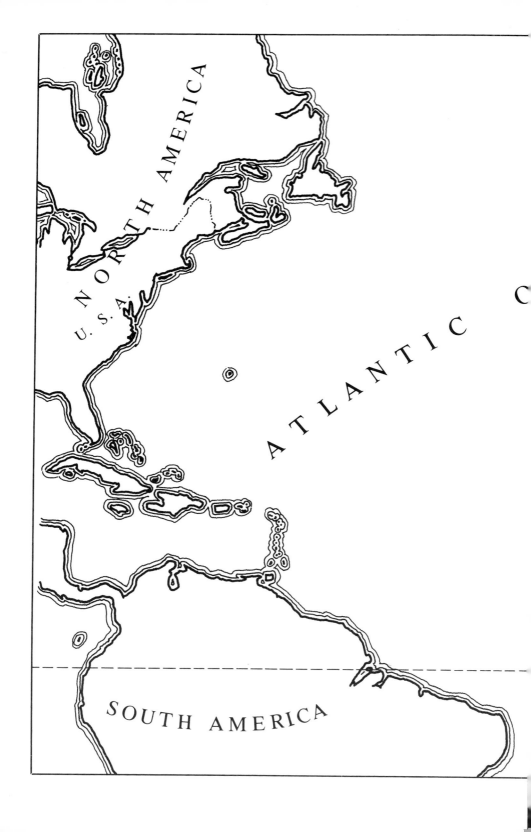

OCEAN

EUROPE

GERMANY

Alsace

FRANCE

AFRICA

Equator

Lambaréné ☆ GABON

Photographs by Erica Anderson
and Others
Design by Charles F. Herrmann, III

Copyright © 1982, 1988 by Ann Cottrell Free
First Edition, 1982
Revised Edition, 1988
Second Printing, 1990
Third Printing, 1991
Fourth Printing, 1993
Fifth Printing, 1994
Sixth Printing, 1995

Library of Congress Catalog Card Number: 88-081164
ISBN 0-9617225-1-7

The Flying Fox Press
4204 Forty-Fifth Street, N.W.
Washington, D.C. 20016

Printed in the United States of America

ANIMALS, NATURE
and
ALBERT SCHWEITZER

Editing and Commentary
Ann Cottrell Free

The Flying Fox Press
Washington, D.C.

Dedicated
to

Rhena Schweitzer Miller

who carries on
the selfless service of her parents,
Hélène Bresslau and Albert Schweitzer

and

to the memory of

Myrta Pearson Ross
1892–1985

Co-founder
The Albert Schweitzer Fellowship

In Memory
of
Dr. Schweitzer's animal companions

To think out in every implication the ethic of love for all creation—this is the difficult task which confronts our age.

— *Albert Schweitzer*

PREFACE

Albert Schweitzer was a man of many talents and purposes—philosopher, physician, musician, theologian, author, builder. His life *was* his argument. And, indeed, it was his monument as well, because he lives on through the accomplishments of the Schweitzer Hospital at Lambaréné, Gabon in Equatorial Africa, through his philosophical works, his studies of Jesus, St. Paul, Goethe and Bach, and through the recorded brilliance of his organ playing.

But perhaps, Albert Schweitzer's most lasting legacy is found in his articulation of his basic philosophy through three words: *reverence for life.* Dr. Schweitzer grappled with the paradoxes of the man-animal-nature relationship as no philosopher had done before. As a result, his philosophy has shaped attitudes, led to passage of laws and, in many ways, has helped to transform the second half of the 20th century.

This small volume—created for all ages—shows, primarily through Dr. Schweitzer's own words, how his philosophy developed as his life unfolded. The book has but one goal: to help keep alive the Albert Schweitzer spirit.

A.C.F.

Man can no longer live for himself alone.
We must realize that all life is valuable and
that we are united to all life. From this
knowledge comes our spiritual relationship
with the universe.

—*Albert Schweitzer*

CONTENTS

CHAPTER ONE
YOUNG SCHWEITZER'S QUESTIONS

Not unlike many children, the young Albert Schweitzer questioned in a child's clear and innocent way the mysterious paradox of life divided against itself.

Not unlike many children, he questioned why his own will to live and to be free of pain should ever be in conflict with the same eager will cherished by a deer, a cow, a pig, a dog, a cat, a horse, a mouse, a bird, a fish—perhaps, even an insect.

But unlike many children, Albert Schweitzer, who was born in 1875, did not lay aside these questions with his playthings as he grew up and left his childhood home in an Alsatian village.

That is why Albert Schweitzer was different. That is why, also, that one day the different may become the usual.

Etched forever in his memory, the sights and sounds of suffering inflicted by man on animals—creatures that had given so much nourishment to the body and soul of man. To the young Schweitzer, this was betrayal.

Many Children Feel This Way

As long as I can remember, I have suffered because of the great misery I saw in the world. I never really knew the artless, youthful joy of living, and I believe that many children feel this way, even when outwardly they seem to be wholly happy and without a single care.
I used to suffer particularly because the poor animals must endure so much pain and want. The sight of an old, limping horse being dragged along by one man while another man struck him with a stick — he was being driven to the Colmar slaughterhouse — haunted me for weeks.

A Prayer

It was quite incomprehensible to me — this was before I began going to school — why in my evening prayers I should pray for human beings only. So when my Mother had prayed with me and had kissed me good-night, I used to add silently a prayer that I had composed for all living creatures. It ran like this:

> *Dear God, protect and bless all living things. Keep them from evil and let them sleep in peace.*

He felt at home with the birds, the deer, and the farm animals in the countryside. One of his earliest ambitions was to be a swineherd—even though the name "Schweitzer" was derived from cow herder.

Even with his intense love of animals and nature, the clergyman's son struggled — not always successfully — with the temptation to conform to the general practices and attitudes toward animals, found not only in his village of Gunsbach, but everywhere. The young Schweitzer found the capacity to resist once he considered the consequences of such actions.

During the holidays I was allowed to act as a driver for our next door neighbor. His chestnut horse was old and broken in wind and it was not good for him to trot much, but in my pride of drivership I gave way again and again to the temptation of whipping him into a trot even though I knew and felt he was tired.... But how my joy disappeared when we got home and I noticed during the unharnessing how the poor animal's flanks were heaving. What good did it do for me to look into his tired eyes and silently ask him to forgive me?

Forgiveness

**Worms
and Fish**

Twice in the company of other boys, I went fishing with a rod. But then my horror at the mistreatment of the impaled worms—and at the tearing of the mouths of the fishes when they were caught—made it impossible for me to continue. Indeed, I even found the courage to dissuade others from fishing.

One Sunday morning during Lent, a friend persuaded the eight-year-old Albert to go out and kill birds with their home-made sling shots.

**Birds
and Bells**

This was a horrible proposal to me, but I dared not refuse for fear he would laugh at me. So we came to a tree which was still bare, and on which the birds were singing out gaily in the morning, without any fear of us. Then stooping over like an Indian on the hunt, my companion placed a pebble in the leather of his sling and stretched it. Obeying his peremptory glance I did the same, with frightful twinges of conscience, vowing firmly that I would not shoot when he did. At that very moment the church bells began to sound, mingling with the song of the

birds in the sunshine. It was the warning bell that came a half-hour before the main bell. For me it was a voice from heaven. I threw the sling down, scaring the birds away, so that they were safe from my companion's sling, and fled home. And ever afterwards when the bells of Holy Week ring out amidst the leafless trees in the sunshine I remember with moving gratitude how they rang into my heart at that time the commandment, "Thou shalt not kill."

Years later reflecting on the incident, Albert Schweitzer realized that particular day marked a turning point in his life.

Freedom

From that day on I have had the courage to free myself from all fear of men. Whenever my deepest convictions were involved I paid less attention than before to the opinions of others. I tried to escape from the dread of being laughed at by my comrades. The great experience of my childhood and youth was the influence of the commandment that we should not kill or torture. All other experiences pale before it.

A Conviction

Out of such heart-breaking experiences that often shamed me there slowly arose in me the unshakable conviction that we had the right to bring pain and death to another being only in case of inescapable necessity, and that all of us must feel the horror that lies in thoughtless torturing and killing. This conviction has become increasingly dominant within me. I have become more and more certain that at the bottom of our hearts we all think so, and simply do not dare to admit it and practice it, because we are afraid that others will laugh at us for being sentimental, and because we have allowed our better feelings to be blunted. But I vowed that I would never let my feelings get blunted, and I would never again fear the reproach of sentimentalism.

When he was ten years old, Albert Schweitzer's parents decided to send him to a preparatory school at Mulhausen in Upper Alsace. There he would live with his aunt and uncle. This meant giving up his two-mile morning and evening walks to and from school at closeby Munster. He credited these walks with awakening his love of nature.

I cried over my lot in secret for hours and hours. I felt as if I were being torn away from nature. To the enthusiasm roused in me by the beauties of nature as I learned to know them on my walks to and from Munster, I tried to give expression in poetry, but I never got further than the first two or three rhymes. Once or twice too, I tried to sketch the hill with the old castle on it which rose from the other side of the valley, but that, too, was a failure. ...Only in musical improvisation have I ever felt myself — as I do still — to have any creative ability.

Torn From Nature

A dreamer during his early student days, Albert Schweitzer found in music, especially the organ — at once tender and majestic — a way to express his feelings about man and nature. A new horizon opened when he met missionaries from Africa, who related stories of unrelieved suffering from injury and disease. And yet another vista opened up. On entering the University of Strasbourg, he discovered science. But he remained vaguely dissatisfied, unable to accept the answers to his questions about the processes of nature.

I t seemed to me laughable that the wind, the rain, the snow, the hail, the formation of the clouds, the spontaneous combustion of hay, the trade winds, the Gulf Stream, thunder and lightning should all have found their proper explanation. The formation of drops of rain, of snowflakes, and of hailstones had always been a special puzzle to me. It hurts me to think that we never acknowledge the absolutely mysterious character of Nature, but always speak so confidently of explaining her, whereas all that we have really done is to go into full and more complicated descriptions which only make the mysterious more mysterious than ever. Even at that age, it became clear to me that Force or "Life" remains in its own essential nature forever inexplicable.

The Mystery of Life

As puzzling as were the riddles of the cosmos, Albert Schweitzer found even more perplexing his own right to health and the promise of a bright future when so many people were mired in ignorance, poverty, and suffering.

Our Share of Misery

Whoever is spared personal pain must feel himself called upon to help in diminishing the pain of others. We must all carry our share of the misery which lies upon the world.

Schweitzer, age 17 with brother Paul.

The path that he followed after leaving the university would have provided most other men and women with great fulfillment. But becoming an acclaimed organist, pastor of a church, principal of a theological seminary, and holder of two doctorates was not enough — not even the authoring of three books, all by the time he was 30 years of age! Thirty was the critical year, for this was the year he was to carry out the secret and momentous decision that he had made when 21 years of age.

A New Path

While still a student, I resolved to devote my life until I was thirty to the office of preacher, to science and to music. If by the time I should have done what I hoped in science and music, I would take a path of immediate service to my fellow man.

He did not know exactly what road he would take, but in 1905, as he reached age 30, he realized the desperate need of the people in the African Congo for medical help. Forthwith, he decided to study medicine so that he could help these victims of disease and foreign exploitation, who, even then, were pressed into forced labor — perhaps slavery. (Schweitzer was unable to forget a statue in an Alsatian town square of a strong, but dejected black African, representative of a people sold in bondage.) He told his astounded congregation at St. Nicholas Church of his decision to give up his European theological career for another in distant Africa.

Atonement

We must make atonement for the terrible crimes we read about in the newspapers. We must make atonement for the still worse ones we do not read about in the papers, crimes that are shrouded in the silence of the jungle night.

A questing, creative, and somewhat non-conformist thinker, Albert Schweitzer hoped, too, that at a distant medical mission he would be free to work out his own theological and philosophical concepts—he would make, therefore, "my life, my argument."

CHAPTER TWO
AFRICA

True to his resolve, Albert Schweitzer followed his plan. At 38, after seven years of educational preparations, he married Helénè Bresslau, who fitted herself for the adventurous task ahead by studying nursing. Sadly leaving behind their Newfoundland dog, Sultan—because of the hot climate ahead—they departed from Europe on March 26, 1913 for Lambaréné in the province of Gabon in French Equatorial Africa. They were accompanied by tremendous boxes of supplies and a piano lined with zinc to withstand the tropical humidity. But Albert Schweitzer had failed to prepare himself for one feature of his life in Africa—the plight of animals in its cities. Not long after he first set foot on the soil of Africa at the port of Dakar, the strong and husky Albert Schweitzer was literally putting his shoulder to the wheel to help animals.

Albert and Helénè Schweitzer

**Pushing
the
Cart**

I have never seen such overworked horses and mules as here. On one occasion when I came upon two natives who were perched on a cart heavily laden with wood which had stuck in the newly mended street, and with loud shouts were belaboring their poor beast, I simply could not pass by, but compelled them to dismount and to push behind till the three of us got the cart on the move.

At Port Gentil, Gabon, Hélène and Albert Schweitzer transferred to an Ogowe River paddle wheeler for the wondrous two-week voyage through the jungle to their final destination.

River and forest...! Who can really describe the first impression they make? We seemed to be dreaming! Pictures of antediluvian scenery which elsewhere had seemed to be merely the creation of fancy, are now seen in real life. It is impossible to say where the river ends and the land begins, for a mighty network of roots, clothed with bright-flowering creepers, projects right into the water. Clumps of palms and palm trees, ordinary trees spreading out widely with green boughs and huge leaves, single trees of the pine family shooting up to a towering height in between them, wide fields of papyrus clumps as tall as a man, with big fan-like leaves, and amid all this luxuriant greenery the rotting stems of dead giants shooting up to heaven.... In every gap in the forest a water mirror meets the eye; at every bend in the river a new tributary shows itself. A heron flies heavily up and then settles on a dead tree trunk; white birds and blue birds skim over the water, and high in the air a pair of ospreys circle. Then — yes, there can be no mistake about it! — from the branch of a palm there hang and swing — two monkey tails! Now the owners of the tails are visible. We are really in Africa!

On arrival at the inland station with its ramshackle buildings and overgrown grounds, he was almost overwhelmed by the primitive conditions and the hot and steamy climate. He converted an abandoned chicken house into a makeshift jungle hospital, but even so, most of the patients arriving from their jungle villages, often with their families, just waited in the open air. They suffered from sleeping sickness, tuberculosis, leprosy, ulcerated and swollen legs, strangulated hernias, malaria and a variety of tropical diseases. Some of his patients were victims of enraged animals they had tried to kill for their meat. Dr. Schweitzer often commented on the protein hunger that drove the natives even into killing hippopotamuses, gorillas, monkeys, and elephants. He had no patience with the old custom of creeping up behind elephants and crippling them by cutting the tendons of their hind legs. And he sorrowed especially over the terrible price hunters exacted from the monkeys for their meat.

One can often bring down or wound three or four in succession and yet never secure their bodies. They get caught among the thick branches or fall into the undergrowth which covers an impenetrable swamp; and if one finds the body, one often finds also a poor little baby monkey, which clings, with lamentations, to its dying mother.

Poor
Little
Baby Monkey

African wildlife appeared to be so plentiful that it was hard to believe that some species could be endangered. But Dr. Schweitzer noticed what was happening to one creature: the white heron.

The White Heron

*U*nfortunately, there are still hunters who pursue the white heron, whose feathers are the most sought after in Europe for hat ornaments. More and more these poor birds are withdrawing into remote and inaccessible stretches of water where they might hope to remain unmolested. They are hardly ever seen now on the river.

The custom of clearing the jungle by fire to make way for cultivation caused him deep sorrow because of the animals trapped within.

Fire

*A*t this time of the year, with the red reflections against the evening sky, I am seized by compassion for the poor beasts that perish in these fires. In ancient China the burning of forests was regarded as a crime, because it meant painful death to so many creatures....

Every day he witnessed the struggle between living and dying.

I *myself am subject to the division of the will-to-live within myself. In a thousand ways my existence is in conflict*

with others. The necessity of taking life and harming life is imposed upon me. When I walk along a lonely path my foot brings pain and death to the tiny forms that populate it. To preserve my life, I must defend it against the life that injures it. I become the persecutor of the little mouse that lives in my house, a murderer of the insect that wants to build its nest there, a mass-murderer of the bacteria that endanger me. I get my food by the destruction of plants and animals. My happiness is built upon injury to my fellow creatures.

Frequently he was called upon to make a choice between "which should live and which should die?"

Choices

From the natives I buy a young fish eagle, which they have caught on a sandbank, in order to rescue it from their cruel hands. But now I must decide whether I shall let it starve, or whether I shall kill a certain number of small fish every day in order to keep it alive. I decide upon the latter course. But every day I find it rather hard to sacrifice — upon my own responsibility — one life for another.

Surrounded by life in its most natural state brought Albert Schweitzer even closer to life's interrelationships and to the perpetual drama and dilemma of the will-to-live versus the will-to-live.

It gave him a new perspective on life, involving him in the slower, timeless rhythms of the jungle, making him more conscious, as he read the newspapers, of "the feverishness and vanity of life" in Europe. That continent's leaders' preoccupation with power politics and material possessions seemed to have alienated them from their natural roots.

It seems almost something abnormal that over a por-   **Man or**
tion of the earth's surface nature should be nothing   **Nature**
and man everything.

Albert Schweitzer in remote Gabon was
not to escape from Europe's growing power
struggle that ushered in the first World War.
Almost immediately he and his wife were
termed enemy aliens by the French. They
were considered German because their once-
French Alsace was, at that time, German. At
first he was forbidden to continue his hospital
work, but soon his medical skills were
needed, regardless of what was considered,
at that moment, his nationality. During this
troubled time, Dr. Schweitzer searched for
the basic reasons driving men and nations to
destruction.

Schweitzer as a civilian intern.

In modern European thought a tragedy is occurring in   **Tragedy**
that the original bonds uniting the affirmative attitude
toward the world with ethics are, by a slow but irresistible
process, loosening and finally parting.

19

What is the nature of this degeneration in our civilization and why has it come about? ...The disastrous feature of our civilization is that it is far more developed materially than spiritually. Its balance is disturbed... Now come the facts to summon us to reflect. They tell us in terribly harsh language that a civilization which develops only on its material side, and not in the sphere of the spirit... heads for disaster.

He examined the philosophies of the Indians and Chinese, concluding that their compassionate views on animals and nature had made little impression on European thought. He wondered why this was so, as the palms rustled "an obbligato to the loud music of the crickets and the toads," pierced at intervals by high-pitched and terrifying cries from the jungle. At his feet, all was peace: a dwarf antelope and his faithful dog, Caramba.

I *n this solitude I try to set in order thoughts which have* **Solitude**
been stirring in me since 1900, in the hope of giving
some little help to the restoration of civilization. Oh solitude
of the primeval forest, how can I ever thank you enough
for what you have been to me?

Clearly, some essential principle was
missing from modern western man's concept
of the world around him—a world he tried to
claim and unmercifully exploit but could
never really own. Could he, Albert Schweitzer,
discover the lost key—or even fashion a new
key—to a more harmonious relationship
between all living things?

F *or months on end I lived in a continual state of men-* **The Iron**
tal turmoil. Without the least success I let my thinking **Door**
become concentrated, even through my daily work at the
hospital, on the real nature of the affirmative attitude and
ethics, and the question of what they have in common. I
was wandering about in a thicket in which no path was to
be found. I was leaning with all my might against an iron
door that would not yield.

The answer that was to unify his thoughts—
and may help to change the world—came
unexpectedly one September day in 1915
while on a slow-moving barge inching up the
Ogowe River, on a mission of mercy, to treat
a missionary's ill wife. It was to be found in a
single phrase, but he did not yet know what
that phrase was to be.

L *ost in thought I sat on the deck of the barge, struggl-* **Struggling**
ing to find the elementary and universal conception
of the ethical which I had not found in any philosophy.
Sheet after sheet I covered with disconnected sentences,
merely to keep myself concentrated on the problem.

Creative forces were at work. Though discouraged, he refused to abandon his writing and crumple up the pages that had borne no fruit.

On the Third Day

Late on the third day, at the very moment, when at sunset, we were making our way through a herd of hippopotamuses, there flashed upon my mind, unforeseen and unsought, the phrase, **"Reverence for Life."** The iron door yielded; the path in the thicket had become visible.

From that moment, Albert Schweitzer was never the same again. The years of searching for a philosophy that could express in a few words his own all-embracing view of life at last had come to an end.

A new challenge lay ahead: The world's acceptance of that philosophy.

CHAPTER THREE
REVERENCE FOR LIFE

Albert and Hélène Schweitzer were repatriated to Europe by the French in 1917 and held as civilian interns. At war's end Albert Schweitzer was in ill health and he underwent surgery. His spirits, for once, were low. Burdened by debts from the old hospital and the need for funds to rebuild and start again, his income came from serving as a Strasbourg hospital physician, a clergyman and concert organist, playing so often the work of his beloved Johann Sebastian Bach, about whom he wrote three books. He lectured at universities in England, Sweden and Switzerland. He also became the father of a daughter, Rhena. Before returning alone to Africa in 1924 to move and rebuild the hospital, he devoted almost full time to completion of four books. In his two-volume *Philosophy of Civilization* he offered, in all of its implications, the meaning of Reverence for Life.

Ethic of Love

I t may seem at first glance as if *Reverence for Life were something too general and too lifeless to provide the content of a living ethic.... Anyone who comes under the influence of Reverence for Life will very soon be able to detect, thanks to what that ethic demands from him, what fire glows in lifeless expression. The ethic of Reverence for Life is the ethic of love widened into universality....*

**Some Sort
of Help**

The ethic of Reverence for Life prompts us to keep each other alert to what troubles us and to speak and act dauntlessly together in discharging the responsibility that we feel. It keeps us watching together for opportunities to bring some sort of help to animals in recompense for the great misery that men inflict upon them, and thus for a moment we escape from the incomprehensible horror of existence.

**Interpreting
Life**

I must interpret the life about me as I interpret the life that is my own. My life is full of meaning to me. The life around me must be full of significance to itself. If I am to expect others to respect my life, then I must respect the other life I see, however strange it may be to mine. And not only other human life, but all kinds of life: life above mine, if there be such life; life below mine, as I know it to exist. Ethics in our Western world has hitherto been largely limited to the relations of man to man. But that is a limited ethics. We need a boundless ethics which will include the animals also.

Dr. Schweitzer concluded that Western ethics in regard to animals and nature had been greatly damaged by the continuing influence of the 17th century French philosopher, René Descartes.

It would seem as if Descartes with his theory that animals have no souls and are mere machines had bewitched all philosophy.

Animal Machines

Because the extension of the principle of love to animal creation means so great a revolution for ethics, philosophy shrinks from this step. It would like to cling to a system of ethics which prescribes for man his behavior toward other men in clear, reasonable commandments without exaggerated demands.

Philosophy Shrinks

As the housewife who has scrubbed the floor sees to it that the door is shut, so that the dog does not come in and undo all her work with his muddy paws, so religious and philosophical thinkers have gone to some pains to see that no animals enter and upset their system of ethics.

Muddy Paws

Philosophy has totally evaded the problem of man's conduct toward other organisms. We might say that it has played a piano of which a whole series of keys were considered untouchable.

Untouchable Keys

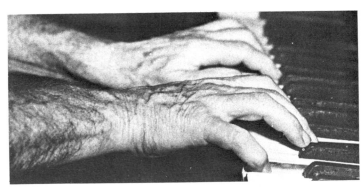

Not all philosophers, of course, had shrunk from the horror of animal suffering. But the influence of the Eastern philosophers and Western defenders, such as Plutarch, St. Francis of Assisi, Jeremy Bentham and Montaigne had not been sufficiently pervasive. The walls of European philosophy, education, religion—excluding animals and nature—continued to stand, even though humane movements were underway in England and the United States. Clearly for Dr. Schweitzer this was insufficient.

Albert Schweitzer looked to the integration of reverence for life into wider teachings of established society. This, he believed, could occur only if there was acceptance that man is part of nature, endowed with the capacity for compassion.

Nature

The deeper we look into nature, the more we realize that it is full of life, and the more profoundly we know that all life is a secret and that we are united with all life that is in nature. Man can no longer live for himself alone. We must realize that all life is valuable and that we are united to all life. From this knowledge comes our spiritual relationship to the universe.

Harsh Mystery

The fact that in nature one creature may cause pain to another, and even deal with it instinctively in the most cruel way, is a harsh mystery that weighs upon us as long as we live. One who has reached the point where he does not suffer ever again because of this has ceased to be a man.

Merciful

How much effort it will take for us to get men to understand the words of Jesus, "Blessed are the merciful," and to bring them to the realization that their responsibility includes all creatures. But we must struggle with courage.

The important thing is that we are part of life. We are born of other lives; we possess the capacities to bring still other lives into existence. In the same way, if we look into a microscope we see cell producing cell. So nature compels us to recognize the fact of mutual dependence, each life necessarily helping the other lives which are linked to it.

Mutual Dependence

Whenever I injure any kind of life I must be quite certain that it is necessary. I must never go beyond the unavoidable, not even in apparently insignificant things. The farmer who has mowed down a thousand flowers in his meadow in order to feed his cows must be careful on his way home not to strike the head off a single flower by the side of the road in idle amusement, for he thereby infringes the law of life without being under the pressure of necessity.

A Single Flower

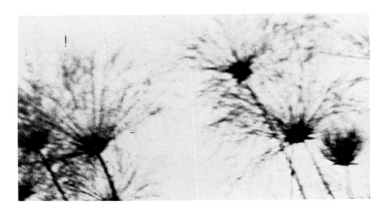

**He Shatters
No Ice
Crystal**

A man is really ethical only when he obeys the constraint laid on him to aid all life which he is able to help, and when he goes out of his way to avoid injuring anything living. He does not ask how far this or that life deserves sympathy as valuable in itself, nor how far it is capable of feeling. To him life as such is sacred. He shatters no ice crystal that sparkles in the sun, tears no leaf from its tree, breaks off no flower, and is careful not to crush any insect as he walks. If he works by lamplight on a summer evening, he prefers to keep the window shut and to breathe stifling air, rather than to see insect after insect fall on his table with singed and sinking wings.

**After
a Rainstorm**

I f he goes out into the street after a rainstorm and sees a worm which has strayed there, he reflects that it will certainly dry up in the sunshine, if it does not quickly regain the damp soil into which it can creep, and so he helps it back from the deadly paving stones into the lush grass. Should he pass by an insect which has fallen into a pool, he spares the time to reach a leaf or stalk on which it may clamber and save itself.

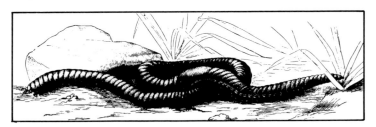

To the man who is truly ethical all life is sacred, includ-ing that which from the human point of view seems lower in the scale. He makes distinctions only as each case comes before him and under the pressure of necessi-ty, as, for example, when it falls to him to decide which of two lives he must sacrifice in order to preserve the other. But all through this series of decisions he is conscious of acting on subjective grounds and arbitrarily, and knows that he bears the responsibility for the life which is sacrificed.

Which Life?

If a life was taken or suffering inflicted because of necessity, Dr. Schweitzer did not forget about it. He would try to make up for that loss.

Whenever an animal is somehow forced into the service of men, every one of us must be concern-ed for any suffering it bears on that account. No one of us may permit any preventable pain to be inflicted, even though the responsibility for that pain is not ours. No one may appease his conscience by thinking that he would be interfering in something that does not concern him. No one may shut his eyes and think the pain, which is there-fore not visible to him, is non-existent.

No One May Shut His Eyes

29

Consolation

*E*ach of us must therefore decide whether to condemn living creatures to suffering and death out of inescapable necessity, and thus incur guilt. Some atonement for guilt can be found by the man who pledges himself to neglect no opportunity to help creatures in distress.

Dr. Schweitzer was often rankled by the low esteem in which animal and nature protectors were held, as if "animal loving" and "nature loving" should automatically mean "people hating," as if all life was created for man's benefit. To him, "life loving" included all.

Nature's Goal?

*W*e like to imagine that man is nature's goal; but the facts do not support that belief.

Often feeling quite isolated from other people because of his beliefs, there were times, however, when he realized he was not alone.

Friend of Nature

*T*he friend of nature is the man who feels himself inwardly united with everything that lives in nature, who shares in the fate of all creatures, helps them when he can in their pain and need, and as far as possible avoids injuring or taking life.

The Masks Fall

*W*e are afraid of shocking people if we let it be noticed how much we are moved by the suffering man brings to animals. We think that others may have become more "rational" than we, and may accept as customary and as a matter of course the things we have gotten excited about. Once in awhile, however, a word suddenly slips out which shows that even they have not yet become reconciled to this suffering. Now they come very close to us though they were formerly strangers. The masks with which we were deceiving each other fall off. Now we learn from each other that no one is able to escape the grip of the cruelty that flourishes ceaselessly around us.

What is often referred to today as "conciousness raising" was expressed simply by Dr. Schweitzer as "thinking." Thinking about our relationship with animals — especially our exploitation — Dr. Schweitzer believed to be a necessity if that exploitation is to be terminated. In short, pure thoughtlessness is the cause of much suffering of animals at the hands of human beings.

The man who has become a thinking being feels a compulsion to give every will-to-live the same reverence for life that he gives to his own. He experiences that other life in his own.

Thinking

He accepts as being good: to preserve life, to promote life, to raise to its highest value life which is capable of development; and as being evil: to destroy life, to repress life which is capable of development. This is the absolute, fundamental principle of the moral, and it is the necessity of thought.

Good and Evil

We must never become callous. When we experience the conflicts ever more deeply we are living in truth. The quiet conscience is an invention of the devil.

The Quiet Conscience

Having lived through World War I and foreseeing another even more dreadful world conflict, Albert Schweitzer appealed to people everywhere to stop and think about the futility of war, how it is born of contempt rather than reverence for all life. He did not forget the animal victims of war — cavalry and artillery horses and mules, carrier pigeons, first aid and scout dogs, and farm animals and pets caught in the line of battle. . . .

**Victims
of
War**

*T*oday there is an absence of thinking which is charac- terized by a contempt for life. We waged war for questions which, through reason, might have been solved. No one won. The war killed millions of men, and brought suffering and death to millions of innocent animals. Why? Because we did not possess the highest rationality of Reverence for Life.

**Extended
Circle**

Albert Schweitzer firmly believed that there could be no peace among members of the human race unless compassion was extended to all creatures.

*U*ntil he extends the circle of his compassion to all living things, man will not himself find peace.

CHAPTER FOUR
DOWN TO CASES

Albert Schweitzer had pronounced views on various specific and often controversial aspects of animal-nature-man relationships. He felt strongly about animals being forced to fight each other or trained to perform for man's amusement.

First among the explanations we hear from lovers of cruel practices is the statement that nature herself is full of cruelty. True — but this does not remove my guilt, when because of my thoughtlessness or delight in the drama of battle, I still further increase the existing measure of woe and suffering.

Nature's Cruelty

It is a disgrace to our time that animal fights are still being staged everywhere, including bull fights and cock fights and other cruel diversions.... In certain southern (European) regions the Sunday pastime consists in giving a rat to a dog in a wire cage. Young and old watch with excitement the vain fight which the rat puts up for its life.

Animal Fights

Performing Animals

The exhibiting of trained animals I abhor. What an amount of suffering and cruel punishment the poor creatures have to endure in order to give a few moments of pleasure to men devoid of all thought and feeling.

Amusements

The time will come when public opinion will no longer tolerate amusements based on the mistreatment and killing of animals. The time will come, but when?

In 1932, he received word in the African jungle that the "romantic sport" of falconry was being revived in Europe.

Falconry

And what is there "romantic" in this sport? Is it that men of an earlier — and in many respects a thoughtless and inhumane — age indulged in it?.... Sport is a physical exercise — not watching a weak creature tortured by a strong one until it falls prey to it.

In keeping with his philosophy of killing only for necessity, Dr. Schweitzer condoned the hunting of animals only if they were destructive to man and crops, but they must be killed as "quickly and painlessly as possible." He could find no excuse for recreational hunting.

*W*hen will we reach the point that hunting, the pleasure of killing animals for sport, will be regarded as a mental aberration?

Sport Hunting

We must reach the point that killing for sport will be felt as a disgrace to our civilization.

To visitors who asked what to do with a young antelope they had purchased from a hunter who had killed its mother, he said, "Unsweetened milk, air, sun, shade and love for the antelope—but what did you do to the hunter?"

Having studied medicine, Albert Schweitzer was well acquainted with the grim life and death of laboratory animals.

Laboratory Animals

Those who experiment upon animals by surgery and drugs, or inoculate them with diseases in order to be able to help mankind by the results obtained, should never quiet their consciences with the conviction that their cruel action may in general have a worthy purpose. In every single instance they must consider whether it is really necessary to demand of an animal this sacrifice for men. And they must take anxious care that the pain be mitigated as far as possible.

While a medical student, he had felt that much of the suffering inflicted on animals was entirely unnecessary.

Pain

How many outrages are committed in scientific institutions where anesthetics are often omitted to save time and trouble? How many also when animals are made to suffer agonizing tortures, only in order to demonstrate to students scientific truths which are perfectly well known?

Expressions of sympathy and calls for greater care, he realized were not enough. (Only the United Kingdom offered any protection to experimental animals.) Until public opinion became stronger and animal substitutes available, Dr. Schweitzer could only take a compensatory spiritual approach toward repayment to these animals for their sacrifice.

The very fact that the animal, as a victim of research has
in his pain rendered such services to suffering men, **Solidarity**
has itself created a new and unique relation of solidarity
between him and ourselves. The result is that a fresh
obligation is laid on each of us to do as much good as we
possibly can to all creatures in all sorts of circumstances.
When I help an insect out of his troubles all that I do is to
attempt to remove some of the guilt contracted through
these crimes against animals.

Dr. Schweitzer was to become aware years
later that United States' public opinion —
encouraged by his concern for animals —
had become more insistent on controls over
laboratory animal suffering along the lines of
the British law. In 1963 he was to express his
approval of legislation introduced in the U.S.
Senate to regulate experimentation in order
to reduce suffering. Heretofore, he had not
involved himself in another nation's law
making processes. But he felt strongly on this
subject.

If you pass such a law in the United States, it will have **Endorsement**
important meaning for the world.

In 1966 the Laboratory Animal Welfare
Act was enacted, but without the specific
pain reduction principles endorsed by Dr.
Schweitzer. Amended three times in 15 years
and now called the Animal Welfare Act, it
primarily regulates acquisition and care of
selected species. Humane groups continue to
press for stronger pain-reduction regulation,
and for further development and use of
viable substitutes for sentient creatures.

Having witnessed the tragic consequences
of uncontrolled breeding of dogs and cats,
Dr. Schweitzer looked to various birth control
measures and euthanasia as the best
solution. In some circumstances obedience to
the command, "not to kill," was false
compassion.

Euthanasia *To put an end by mercy killing to the suffering of a creature, when that suffering cannot be alleviated, is more ethical than to stand aloof from it.*

Dr. Schweitzer carried out the law of "necessity" in his control of life-threatening tropical insects and snakes. But as his philosophical and biological perceptions deepened, he tried to be more discriminating, allowing, for example, a non-threatening column of ants to cross his path rather than destroying them by fire or chemicals. He searched for more natural biological controls to reduce dependence on certain chemical pesticides as he learned of their toxic effects on man and nature. Rather than treating pilings with chemicals to resist termites, he discovered a termite-proof wood. Within the rooms assigned to staff and visitors, there was posted, not without humor, a long list of "do's and dont's." No. 10 on the list:

Do not use insecticides for killing the poor creatures. **Poor**
Invite them to take a walk in nature. Insecticides **Creatures**
are dangerous for your health.

From his earliest years, Albert Schweitzer
was deeply moved by conditions that prevailed
in the handling and slaughtering of animals
used for meat.

Let no one regard as light the burden of his responsibi- **Animals**
lity. While so much ill-treatment of animals goes on, **Into**
while the moans of thirsty animals in railway trucks sound **Meat**
unheard, while so much brutality prevails in our slaughter
houses, while animals have to suffer in our kitchens pain-
ful death from unskilled hands, while animals have to en-
dure intolerable treatment from heartless men . . . we all
bear guilt for it.

In the years since Dr. Schweitzer wrote
those words, many Western nations have
passed humane slaughter laws. Nevertheless

in many parts of the world, much slaughter brutality continues. Rough handling, especially in highway trucking continues to be widespread. Slaughter improvements, however, have been followed with a new and dubious kind of animal-raising, known as the "factory farm."

As Dr. Schweitzer's perceptions and convictions deepened, he discontinued consumption of meat. Erica Anderson, his biographer, wrote in 1965:

"No bird or animal in the hospital village—hen or pig or sheep—is killed for food. Fish and crocodile meat brought by fishermen are occasionally served at table, but Schweitzer himself in recent years has given up eating either meat or fish, even the liver dumplings he used to relish and enjoy. 'I can't eat anything that was alive any more.' When a man questioned him on his philosophy and said that God made fish and fowl for people to eat, he answered, 'Not at all.'"

During his final illness in 1965, his daughter, Rhena, suggested beef broth. He declined.

CHAPTER FIVE
ANIMALS AND PLANTS AROUND HIM

Life without animals around him was, for Dr. Schweitzer, scarcely a life worth living. He recorded their comings, goings and life events in his diary-scrapbooks along with those of his human friends. (A distressed Dr. Schweitzer lived only seven months after authorities ordered the destruction of his dogs, cats and monkeys because of the fear of rabies.)

Dr. Schweitzer was not without his favorites among his companion animals, appreciating not only their intelligence, but certain attributes of character usually ascribed to human beings.

And let us not forget that some of the more evolved animals show that they have feelings and are capable of impressive, sometimes amazing acts of fidelity and devotion.   **Animal Feelings**

Schweitzer with Sultan

From the very first, back home in Alsace, there were dogs, such as Phylax and Sultan. In Lambaréné, over the years there were many favorites: Caramba, Amos, Porto, Hannibal, Cesar, Kimmy, and especially the white and tan mixed terrier, Tchu Tchu. She was the only dog allowed in the dining room, thus becoming the beneficiary of table tidbits.

Likewise, the cats played an important role in his life—even a domineering one. Sizi sat on his desk as he wrote, often falling asleep

on his left arm, which, of course, he dared not move. This went on for 23 years. Sizi had been rescued by Dr. Schweitzer when she was a kitten after he heard her plaintive "meow" under the floor of a building under construction. (He was constantly expanding his village, making room for more patients, their families, and for the increasing number of doctors and nurses.)

Another cat, Piccolo, took her siestas on papers piled on Dr. Schweitzer's desk. Should they be in urgent need of his signature for immediate dispatch, well, too bad.

The more exotic animal companions (that is, exotic to Europeans) were the native monkeys, gorillas, chimpanzees, pelicans, antelope. Monkeys abounded.

Monkeys and More Monkeys

I have the virtue of caring for all stray monkeys that come to our gate. (If you have had any experience with large monkeys, you know why I say it is a virtue thus to take care of all comers until they are old enough or strong enough to be turned loose, several together, in the forest — a great occasion for them — and for me!) Sometimes there will come to our monkey colony a wee baby monkey whose mother has been killed, leaving this orphaned infant. I must find one of the older monkeys to adopt and care for the baby. I never have any difficulty about it, except to decide which candidate shall be given the responsibility. Many a time it happens that the seemingly worst-tempered monkeys are most insistent upon having this sudden burden of foster parenthood given to them.

One of these monkeys was cared for by his Canadian friend and translator, Mrs. C.E.B. Russell. They called the monkey "Canada." Once, when Dr. Schweitzer and Mrs. Russell were in St. Nicholas Church in Strasbourg, Alsace, Dr. Schweitzer concluded a private organ concert of several Bach preludes and fugues with an improvised offering to the far-distant "Canada." For them both, wrote Mrs. Russell, it brought back Africa.

"So he proceeded to improvise more beautifully **Magic**
than I have ever heard him before or since. It **Music**
was all full of the magic of the African forest, the moon-
light in the jungle and on the river, the merry gambols of
the monkeys in the trees when the sun is shining. . . ."

Orphaned or injured young gorillas and
chimpanzees presented more of a problem.
Most of these were brought to the hospital
village by hunters (not necessarily out of
sympathy since they usually had killed their
mothers) because they knew that Dr.
Schweitzer would reimburse them, as he did
all who brought other helpless young creatures
to him.

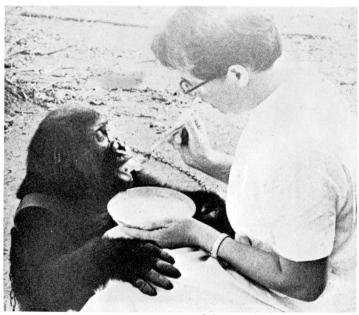
Schweitzer's daughter, Rhena.

Raised like children — especially the
chimpanzee, Fifi, and gorillas, Penelope and
Peter — they became too strong and
unpredictable to live free in the compound.
They were too unsophisticated in the ways of
the jungle to be returned to the wild.

Regretfully, the only alternative: zoological gardens. In all, thirteen gorillas went to zoos from Lambaréné. They were accompanied sometimes by a Lambaréné friend such as Dr. Schweitzer's daughter, Rhena, to help make the trip and transition easier.

He was especially partial to gorillas. But he advised all who entered the forest territory of these powerful (now increasingly rare) primates to treat them with utmost respect.

The intelligence and close resemblance of pigs to human beings was not wasted on Dr. Schweitzer. He gave a home to a series of Red River hogs—all called Thekla, for an obscure operatic character. The first Thekla was brought to the hospital compound as a scrawny piglet. Not only did she respond in weight gain to tender loving care, she became something of a "problem child." Mischievous, she seized every opportunity to become a one-pig hurricane: romping about madly, knocking against doctors, nurses, furniture, killing chickens, even snatching food from patients and their families. Threats were made on her life. Penning up did no good. She would dig out. Reluctantly, Dr. Schweitzer sent her to the London Zoo. When he visited her there years later, he called her name and she recognized him. Clearly, the loss of Thekla left an empty space in his heart. As he had to her, he often sang succeeding young Theklas to sleep with the gentle Brahms Lullaby.

Music and animals merged time and time again, most pronouncedly so with the arrival of three orphaned fledgling pelicans—brought in for money by the hunter who killed their mother. They were named for the German composer, Richard Wagner's legendary Tristan, Lohengrin and Parsifal. As soon as they were trained to live as pelicans, two of them joined passing pelicans and flew away—but not Parsifal. He decided to become

Dr. Schweitzer's night watchman, taking up his perch outside the doctor's quarters, permitting no one to pass. He became such a presence at the hospital that Dr. Schweitzer wrote a small book, *A Pelican Talks About His Life,* in which Parsifal tells his life story. If "M. le Pelican," as he came to be known, was a formidable presence, more so, a turkey who guarded the lane to the outdoor toilet, pecking at the legs of passersby.

Dr. Schweitzer asked people entering the hospital village by car to respect the ducks, geese and chickens. He erected a large sign with their pictures and the admonition to "Drive slowly." He always carried in his pocket a very small cloth bag of grain and rice so that he could pause and feed various fowl. This could have been the reason that one red hen took a special fancy to Dr. Schweitzer. She even insisted on spending the night in his room, but when she decided to bring a chicken friend, Dr. Schweitzer shooed them both away.

Among the gentlest and most beloved of
his animal companions were the graceful
antelope, each raised from infancy and
housed close to Dr. Schweitzer's living
quarters. The list was long: Lucie, Leonie,
Theodore, Pamela, Caro, Erica—each an
individual. During his later years, he would
often take an evening stroll with Leonie and
Theodore.

Dr. Schweitzer often mentioned that
having so many animals at Lambaréné
served some practical purposes, as well as
providing amusement such as the sight of a
goat using a cellar door as a sliding board.
The animals supplied valuable fertilizer for
enriching the earth.

Not a day passed that Dr. Schweitzer did not spare some small non-human life—just as he saved the lives and eased the pain of patients. A bee that mistakenly had flown indoors would be captured by an inverted drinking glass, a cardboard slipped beneath it, and released. He would step aside rather than needlessly crush an ant, a beetle, a worm. When tadpoles were left in small pools— separated from the river on the receding tide—he would open up a passageway to take them back to the river.

False Distinctions

In the past we have tried to make a distinction between animals which we acknowledge have some value and others which, having none, can be liquidated when we wish. This standard must be abandoned. Everything that lives has value simply as a living thing, as one of the manifestations of the mystery that is life.

When constructing new buildings, Dr. Schweitzer was careful to avoid injury to small creatures that might be in the way. A hospital built to save lives certainly should not be built on a foundation of death and suffering.

Small Creatures

Before the pile is lowered in the hole, I always look to see whether any ants or toads or other creatures have fallen into it. And if so, I take them out with my hands, that they may not be crushed by the pile or later killed by the pounding down of earth and stones.

50

This consideration—so far as practicable—extended to all other life forms: flowers, plants, trees. The only real pleasure he received from floral tributes sent him frequently when abroad was derived from the kind thoughts behind the gesture. In Lambaréné he advised patients, staff and visitors not to cut the flowers. Not only would he move a new road to save an orange tree, he once transplanted a grove of palm trees.

Extra Work

We burden ourselves with some extra work out of compassion for the palm trees with which the site of our future home is crowded. The simplest plan would be to cut them all down. An oil palm is valueless, there are so many of them. But we cannot find it in our heart to deliver them over to the axe just when delivered of the creeper vines, they are beginning a new life. So we devote some of our leisure hours to digging up carefully those which are transplantable and setting them elsewhere, though it is heavy work. . . .

Dr. Schweitzer lived his philosophy each day of his life. Whenever called on to make a life or death judgment, he considered each case separately, always hoping that the continuation of life could be justified.

Nature was constantly repaying man, Dr. Schweitzer believed, by offering its own beauty to lift the sorrowful heart. For those persons seeing only the dark side of life, Albert Schweitzer had a few words:

Beauty

Never say there is nothing beautiful in the world anymore. There is always something to make you wonder in the shape of a tree, the trembling of a leaf.

Deep Roots

A tree grows, bears fruit—then, after a certain time, it no longer grows, it loses its leaves, its branches wither. What happens? Why is its vital energy checked? Because it did not sink deep enough roots into the earth on which it stands. Anyone who has to do with trees knows what I mean. The same thing—I thought to myself—has happened with us humans. Humanity has not had deep enough roots. It has not found sustenance and fresh impetus, because the ethical code on which it was based was too narrow and did not have a deep foundation. It has concerned itself only with human beings. It has given only a passing nod to our relationship with other living creatures, looking upon it as a nice bit of sentimentality, quite innocuous but of no great significance. But it did have significance. For only if we have an ethical attitude in our thinking about all living creatures does our humanity have deep roots and a rich flowering that cannot wither.

CHAPTER SIX
THE WORLD LISTENS

During the dark years of World War II, Dr. Schweitzer remained at Lambaréné, short-staffed and under-supplied, relying on supportive groups, particularly the Albert Schweitzer Fellowship in the United States. He emerged from Africa in 1948 to a wounded, changed and changing world. Victors and vanquished alike looked to Dr. Schweitzer's philosophy for the restoration of hope and sanity.

In 1952, he was chosen for the Nobel Peace Prize in recognition of his humanitarianism. There could be no peace, he said in his acceptance speech, no harmony among men and nations unless prejudice and nationalism were laid aside, and all humankind recognized and embraced the universality of life — specifically, "all living creatures."

The human spirit is not dead: It lives on in secret.... It has come to believe that compassion, in which all ethics must take root, can only attain its full breadth and depth if it embraces all living creatures and does not limit itself to mankind.   **Compassion**

Little that Dr. Schweitzer pointed to in those postwar years showed more clearly the interrelationship between man and nature than the effect on man and the biosphere of continued nuclear testing.

Warning of the insidious effects on generations of unborn children for centuries to come, his voice and those of thousands of scientists were heard by many governments that ceased their open-air nuclear testing.

Nuclear Fall-out

The radioactive elements released in the air by nuclear tests do not stay there permanently. In the form of radioactive rain and radioactive snow they fall down on the earth. They enter the plants through leaves and roots and stay there. We absorb them through the plants, by drinking milk from the cows or by eating the meat of animals which have fed on them. Radioactive rain infects our drinking water.

More Americans became aware of Dr. Schweitzer when in 1949, at age 74, he made his first trip to the United States to pay homage to one of the greatest influences on his life, the poet-dramatist, Johann Wolfgang von Goethe, whose 200th anniversary was being celebrated at Aspen, Colorado. His debt to Goethe was profound.

What binds us together in the deepest depths of our   **Goethe**
being is his [Goethe] philosophy of nature.

Perhaps the most heartening moment
during his trip was the sight from his train
window of bales of hay being dropped from
airplanes to hungry deer gathered in an
inaccessible valley. *"Reverence for Life,"* he
called out, *"Vive l'Amerique!"*

Dr. Schweitzer's philosophy opened a new
dimension to the struggling world of North
American animal welfare, becoming especially
noticeable in the early 1950's. For then,
there came into being the Animal Welfare
Institute, the Society for Animal Protective
Legislation, The Humane Society of the
United States and the Kindness Club in
Canada.

In most communities, humane societies — if such existed — struggled to make ends meet, their efforts often denigrated. But now they saw a leader: at last, a world figure, unafraid to speak up for animals. Encouraged, they took their fight for stronger animal protection to court houses, legislatures and to Washington's Capitol Hill. In the years following Dr. Schweitzer's presence in the United States — when there were only two animal protective Federal laws on the statute books — soon one after another was to be enacted. It was not easy. Bitter struggles ensued and continue today in the effort to seek broader coverage and better enforcement. Dr. Schweitzer clearly realized that the tide had turned.

In 1954 the Animal Welfare Institute presented to Dr. Schweitzer a gold replica of its Albert Schweitzer medal, awarded nearly every year thereafter for outstanding service to animals. On it, his image with his dog, Tchu Tchu, and his words:

Boundless Ethics

W*e need a boundless ethics which will include the animals also.*

56

In giving his permission to strike the medal, Dr. Schweitzer wrote to "my companion in the struggle," AWI president, Christine Stevens:

I *am profoundly moved that you would like to give my name to the medal you have created. I give you this right with all my heart. I would never have believed that my philosophy, which incorporates in our ethics a compassionate attitude toward all creatures, would be noticed and recognized in my lifetime. I knew this truth would impose itself one day on human thought, but it is the great and moving surprise of my life that I should still be able to witness this progress of ethics.*

Moving Surprise

Had he lived a few years longer, he would have been astounded that the momentum had not flagged, with more persons becoming aware of the atrocities condoned by custom, greed and ignorance—and demanding "why?"

Calls continue to mount for an immediate halt to trapping, fur "ranching", painful laboratory procedures, factory farming. And efforts are also moving forward on many fronts to educate the young on man's inconsistent ethical attitude toward animals and to show that animals deserve their rights in a world dominated by humans. This may lead to a new, more humane way of thinking. Dr. Schweitzer strongly felt that youth held the key, writing this advice to teachers:

Heart and Reason

Start early to instill in your students an awareness that they are on this earth to help and serve others.... May it be the good fortune of this school to have teachers who not only pass on knowledge to the children on the road of life, but who also give them the deep realization that the heart must always play its part as well as reason.

On becoming honorary president of the Kindness Club, he wrote, in 1959, its Canadian founder, Aida Flemming, lamenting the "dreadful play" of uninstructed children with helpless animals. He welcomed her aspirations to inspire to a "new humanity":

A New Humanity

Our civilization lacks humane feeling. We are humans who are insufficiently humane! We must realize that and seek to find a new spirit. We have lost sight of this ideal because we are solely occupied with thoughts of men instead of remembering that our goodness and compassion should extend to all creatures. Religion and philosophy have not insisted as much as they should on the fact that our kindness should include all living creatures.... The pages that you sent me tell me that you also are seized with this idea. I am greatly impressed by your letter. I am profoundly moved, because we aspire to a new humanity.

From Japan in 1961 came the request that he serve the Japanese Animal Welfare Society as an honorary patron. In his acceptance, he wrote:

Any religion or philosophy which is not based on a respect for life is not a true religion or philosophy.

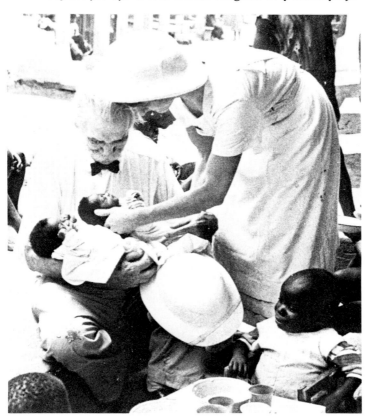

The world in the post-war years seemed to be "beating a path" to Dr. Schweitzer's Lambaréné door, so inspired were the volunteer physicians, nurses, technicians, theologians, philosophers, journalists by the example of this selfless, many-faceted man. Sometimes "le grand docteur" would disappoint them by talking at length about his animals instead of the great issues of the day!

59

On occasion, he discouraged his admirers from coming to the now greatly expanded Lambaréné hospital and village, reminding them that their services probably could be used more effectively at home or elsewhere. He told them:

Everyone has his Lambaréné.

Making her own Lambaréné in Silver Spring, Maryland, near Washington, D.C., was Rachel Carson as she labored, though weakening from cancer, to alert the world to the dangers of misuse of certain "miracle" pesticides, just as had Dr. Schweitzer warned on the dangers of nuclear contamination. She dedicated her 1962 book *Silent Spring* to Dr. Schweitzer, using his own words:

Capacity to Foresee

Man has lost the capacity to foresee and forestall. He will end by destroying the earth.

Learning of the destruction of a French apiarist's honeybees due to indiscriminate spraying of new post World War II chemical insecticides, Dr. Schweitzer, noting their effect on the chain of life, wrote the bee keeper:

To a Bee Keeper

I am aware of some of the tragic repercussions of the chemical fight against insects taking place in France and elsewhere, and I deplore them. Modern man no longer knows how to foresee or to forestall. He will end by destroying the earth from which he and other living creatures draw their food. Poor bees, poor birds, poor men. . . .

The great environmental awakening began with *Silent Spring.* (Soon, in the United States there was a public demand for a National Environmental Policy Act. In Schweitzerian fashion, this 1969 Act required any government agency planning to alter the environment to justify, in detail, the action's necessity.)

Rachel Carson

On receiving the Albert Schweitzer Medal in 1962, Rachel Carson called Dr. Schweitzer "the one truly great individual our modern times have produced." She said: "If during the coming years we are to find our way through the problems that beset us, it will surely be in large part through the wider understanding and application of his principles."

Albert Schweitzer was never to meet some of those humanitarians and naturalists whom he influenced the most, for he had returned permanently to Africa in 1959, leaving behind forever the hills of Alsace, where nature first "spoke" to him.

A Longer Journey

Now I have left the mountains and the castles and the woods. I stand before the church and see the swallows once more. The swallows are gathering for the journey south. We will set out together. But a time will come when I will not see you when you gather for this journey, and you will set out for the south without me, for I will have gone on a longer journey from one world to another.

Albert Schweitzer died at age 90 on September 4, 1965, at Lambaréné, realizing that attitudes were changing. He had the satisfaction of knowing that by persistently seeking answers to his boyhood questions, he had given guidance to those whose hearts were lacerated by animal suffering and the ravaging of nature. But he had no way of knowing that in coming years philosophers and thoughtful men and women everywhere would no longer shrink from confronting the last unacknowledged right: the right of an animal—or even a tree—(communicating through the conscience of man) to say "No." Nor could Dr. Schweitzer know that a new and different future for exploited animals and nature was evolving, largely because of him. But by looking to the past, he was well aware that no revolutionary truth is acceptable to the majority when it is first introduced.

The Fate of Every Truth

I t is the fate of every truth to be an object of ridicule when it is first acclaimed. It was once considered foolish to suppose that black men were really human beings and ought to be treated as such. What was once foolish has now become a recognized truth. Today it is considered as exaggeration to proclaim constant respect for every form of life as being the serious demand of a rational ethic. But the time is coming when people will be amazed that the human race existed so long before it recognized that thoughtless injury to life is incompatible with real ethics. Ethics is in its unqualified form extended responsibility with regard to everything that has life.

As his life unfolded, Albert Schweitzer steadily grew into his ideals. It was not always easy. But he was convinced that others could do likewise once they gave serious thought to the possibility of breaking away from the tyranny of cultural custom and personal habit.

*V*ery little of the great cruelty shown by men can real- **Let Us**
ly be attributed to cruel instinct. Most of it comes from **Work**
thoughtlessness or inherited habit. The roots of cruelty,
therefore, are not so much strong as widespread. But the
time must come when inhumanity protected by custom and
thoughtlessness will succumb before humanity championed
by thought. Let us work that this time may come.

Albert Schweitzer realized that even his
deepest concentration could not solve the
puzzle that dominated his life since
childhood: *I am life which wills to live in the*
midst of life which wills to live. But he came
to a kind of terms with the mystery and
showed others how they could do likewise:
Make judgments with a prayerful and
humble heart, realizing that love cannot be
compartmentalized. It embraces all life.

*T*o think out in every implication the ethic of love for **For All**
all creation — this is the difficult task which confronts **Creation**
our age.

CHRONOLOGY

January 14, 1875—Albert Schweitzer born at Kayserberg, Alsace* to Adele Schillinger Schweitzer and Lutheran Pastor, Louis Schweitzer.

1880-1884—Attended village school, Gunsbach.

1885-1893—Student at gymnasium, Mulhausen.

1893 —Began studies, University of Strasbourg; also studied organ in Paris.

April 1894-April 1895—Served required military service.

1896-1899—Studied at Sorbonne and University of Berlin; also studied organ in Paris and Berlin. Began giving concerts. Published first book.

1899—Received doctorate of philosophy, University of Strasbourg.

1900—Received a licentiate degree in theology; ordained as curate.

January 14, 1905—Age 30; made decision to study medicine and go to Africa.

1906. Began medical studies, University of Strasbourg.

1912. Married Hélène Bresslau.

1913. Completed internship and received M.D. degree. Left for Africa.

1914-17—Considered enemy alien by French authorities, but could continue medical practice.

September, 1915—After years of searching, he finds the words, *Reverence for Life,* that sum up his philosophy.

1917—The Schweitzers transferred to France as civilian interns.

1918—Returned to Alsace in poor health.

1919-1923—Daughter born, recovered health, lectured widely, practiced medicine, gave organ concerts, preached, wrote and published books, including the two-volume *Philosophy of Civilization.*

1924-1927—Returned to Africa; rebuilt hospital at new location.

1927-1939—Made several trips to and from Africa. Lectured widely and played organ throughout Europe.

1939-1948—Remained in Lambaréné during World War II. Mrs. Schweitzer joins him after hazardous escape from Europe.

1949. First and only trip to the United States.

1954—Accepts in Oslo, Norway the 1952 Nobel Peace Prize and gold replica of the Albert Schweitzer Medal of the Animal Welfare Institute.

May 30, 1957—Death of Hélène Schweitzer in Switzerland.

1958-1963—Worked for nuclear test ban treaty. Period of great expansion at hospital. He has become one of the world's leading citizens.

May 6, 1963—Endorsed a U.S. Senate bill to reduce laboratory animal suffering.

March, 1965— His dogs, cats and monkeys put to death by authorities.

September 4, 1965—Died at Lambaréné. Age 90.

*Alsace—often referred to as Alsace-Lorraine—is today a region of northeastern France located on the German border. Since the 4th century the area has passed back and forth between France and Germany and their tribal predecessors.

SOURCES FOR SELECTIONS

Chapter One: The Young Schweitzer's Questions

2. Many Children. *The Animal World of Albert Schweitzer.* Edited by Charles R. Joy. Boston: Beacon Press, 1950, p. 44. Hereinafter referred to as *Animal/Joy.* (Selection translated by Joy from *Aus Meiner Kindheit und Jugendzeit.* Hereinafter referred to as *Kindheit.*)

2. A Prayer. *Albert Schweitzer: Thoughts for Our Times.* Edited by Erica Anderson. Mount Vernon, N.Y.: Peter Pauper Press, 1975, p. 9. (Selection translated by Anderson from *Kindheit.*)

3. Forgiveness. *Memoirs of Childhood and Youth,* by Albert Schweitzer. Translated by C.T. Campion from *Kindheit.* New York: Macmillan, 1955, p. 30. (Hereinafter referred to as *Memoirs/*Campion.)

4. Worms and Fish. *Animal/*Joy, op. cit., p. 46. From *Kindheit.*

4. Birds and Bells. Ibid., p. 44. (Translation correction, line 9, — inclusion of "not" — by Antje Lemke.)

5. Freedom. Ibid., p. 44.

6. A Conviction. Ibid., p. 46.

7. Torn From Nature. *Memoirs/*Campion, op. cit., p. 22.

7. Mystery of Life. Ibid., p. 52.

8. Our Share of Misery, Ibid., p. 61.

9. A New Path. Ibid., p. 61.

10. Atonement. *Reverence for Life: Sermons of Albert Schweitzer.* Translated by Reginald Fuller. New York: Harper and Row, 1969, pp. 56-57.

Chapter Two: Africa

12. Pushing the Cart. *On the Edge of the Primeval Forest and More From the Primeval Forest,* by Albert Schweitzer. Translated by C.T. Campion from *Zwishen Wasser und Urwald und Das Spittal im Urwald.* New York: Macmillan, p. 11. (Hereinafter referred to as *Edge/More.*)

13. Two Monkey Tails. Ibid., p. 15.

15. Poor Little Baby Monkey. Ibid., p. 49.

16. The White Heron. *Animal/*Joy, op. cit., p. 16. Translated by Charles Joy from *Afrikanische Jagdegeschichichten.*

16. *Fire. Albert Schweitzer: An Anthology.* Edited by Charles R. Joy. Boston: Beacon Press. 1947, p. 279. (Hereinafter referred to as *Anthology*/Joy.) From *Living Age,* Sept. 1938.

17. Constant Struggle. *Animal*/Joy, op. cit., p. 189. Translated by Joy From *Kultur und Ethik.*

18. Choices. *Out of My Life and Thought,* by Albert Schweitzer. Translated by C.T. Campion from *Aus Meinen Leben und Denken.* New York: Henry Holt, 1949, p. 234. (Hereinafter referred to as *Life.*)

19. Man or Nature. *Edge/More,* op. cit., p. 101.

19. Tragedy. *Life,* op. cit., p. 153.

20. Questions. *Philosophy of Civilization;* Part II *Civilization and Ethics,* by Albert Schweitzer. Translated by C.T. Campion from *Kultur und Ethik.* New York: Macmillan, 1949. Reprint, University Presses of Florida, 1981, p. 86.

21. Solitude. *Edge/More,* op. cit., p. 100

21. Iron Door. *Life.* op. cit., p. 155.

21. Struggling. Ibid., p. 155.

22. Third Day. Ibid., p. 156

Chapter Three: Reverence for Life

23. Ethic of Love. *Out of My Life and Thought,* p. 232.

24. Some Sort of Help. *Animal*/Joy, op. cit., p. 191. From *Kultur.*

24. Interpreting Life. Ibid., p. 30. From *Kultur.*

25. Animal Machines. *The Teaching of Reverence for Life,* by Albert Schweitzer. Translated by Richard and Clare Winston. New York: Holt, Rinehart and Winston. 1965, pp. 49-50). (Hereinafter referred to as *Teaching.*)

25. Philosophy Shrinks. *Animal*/Joy, op. cit., p. 187. From the *International Journal of Animal Protection,* Edinburgh: May 1935. (Hereinafter referred to as *Journal.*)

25. Muddy Paws. *Teaching,* op. cit., p. 49.

25. Untouchable Keys. Ibid., p. 50.

26. Nature. *Anthology*/Joy, op. cit., p. 248. From *Christian Century,* vol. 51, 1934.

26. Harsh Mystery. *Animal*/Joy, op. cit., p. 177. From *Atlantis,* Zurich, 1932.

26. Harsh Mystery. *Animal*/Joy, op. cit., p. 190. From *Atlantis*, Zurich, 1932.

26. Merciful. Letter to James Sinclair, Franklin, LA, June 14, 1959. (Ref. Matthew, V, 7).

27. Mutual Dependence. Ibid., p. 272. From *Christendom*, vol. 1, no. 1, 1936.

27. A Single Flower. *Animal*/Joy, op. cit., p. 190. From *Kultur*.

28. He Shatters No Ice Crystal. *Philosophy of Civilization;* Part II, *Civilization and Ethics*, by Albert Schweitzer. Translated by John Naish from *Kultur und Ethik*. London: A & C Black, 1923, p. 254. (Hereinafter referred to as *Civilization*/Naish.)

28. After a Rainstorm. Ibid., p. 254.

29. Which Life? *Life*, op. cit., p. 253.

29. No One May Shut His Eyes. *Animal*/Joy, op. cit., p. 191. From *Kultur*.

30. Consolation. *Teaching*, op. cit., p. 23.

30. Nature's Goal. *Anthology*/Joy, op. cit., p. 252. From *Christian Century*.

30. Friend of Nature. *Animal*/Joy, op. cit., p. 177.

30. Masks Fall. Ibid., p. 191. From *Kultur*.

31. Thinking. *Life*, op. cit., p. 158.

31. Good and Evil. Ibid., p. 158.

31. Quiet Conscience. *Animal*/Joy, op. cit., p. 190. From *Kultur*.

32. Victims of War. *Anthology*/Joy, op. cit., p. 260. From *Christendom*.

32. Extended Circle. *Civilization*/Naish, op. cit.

Chapter Four: Down to Cases

33. Nature's Cruelty. *The Animal World of Albert Schweitzer*, Joy, p. 177. From *Atlantis*.

33. Animal Fights. Ibid., p. 178.

34. Performing Animals. *Memoirs*/Campion, op. cit., p. 31.

34. Amusements. *Teaching*, op. cit., p. 50.

34. Falconry. *Animal*/Joy, op. cit., p. 177. From *Atlantis*.

35. Sport Hunting, *Teaching*, op. cit., p. 50.

36. Laboratory Animals. *Animal.*/Joy, op. cit., p. 190. From *Kultur*.

37. Pain. *Civilization*/Naish, op. cit., p. 264.

37. Solidarity. Ibid., p. 264.

37. Endorsement. Letter to U.S. Senator Maurine Neuberger of Oregon May 6, 1963.

38. Euthanasia. *Indian Thought and Its Development,* by Albert Schweitzer. Translated by Mrs. C.E.B. Russell from *Die Weltanschuauung der indischen Denken,* New York: Henry Holt. 1936, p. 83.

39. Poor Creatures. Unpublished memorandum.

39. Animals Into Meat. *Civilization*/Naish, op. cit., p. 253.

40. *The Schweitzer Album,* by Erica Anderson. New York: Harper and Row. 1965, p. 37.

Chapter Five: Animals And Plants Around Him

41. Animal Feelings. *The Schweitzer Album,* by Erica Anderson. New York: Harper and Row, 1965. p. 42. (Hereinafter referred to as *Album*/Anderson.)

44. Monkeys and More Monkeys. *Anthology*/Joy, op. cit., p. 282. From *Christendom.*

45. Magic Music. *Animal*/Joy, p. 26.

50. False Distinctions. *Album*/Anderson, op. cit., p. 42.

50. Small Creatures. *Edge/More,* op. cit., p. 112.

51. Extra Work. *Edge/More,* op. cit., p. 157.

51. Beauty. *Album*/Anderson, op. cit., p. 39.

52. Deep Roots. *Schweitzer Album,* ibid., p. 44.

Chapter Six: The World Listens

53. Compassion. Nobel Peace Prize address: *The Problem of Peace in the World Today.* New York: Harper and Row, 1954. Reprinted, *The Courier,* Albert Schweitzer Fellowship, April, 1978, p. 12.

54. Nuclear Fall-out. *Peace or Atomic War?* New York: Holt, Rinehart and Winston, 1958. p. 8. (Three broadcasts from Oslo.)

55. Goethe. Albert Schweitzer. *Goethe—Five Studies.* Translated by Charles R. Joy. Boston. Beacon Press. 1961. p. 3.

56. Boundless Ethics. *Animal*/Joy, op. cit., p. 30.

57. Moving Surprise. Letter to Christine Stevens.

58. Heart and Reason. *Humane Education* Magazine. The Humane Society of the United States. Spring, 1978.

58. A New Humanity. Letter to Aida Flemming.

59. True Religion. Letter to Japanese Animal Welfare Society.

60. Capacity to Foresee. *Silent Spring*, by Rachel Carson. Boston: Houghton Mifflin, 1962.

61. To A Bee Keeper. *Bulletin,* Dec., 1956, International Union for the Conservation of Nature and Natural Resources, Brussels, Belgium.

62. A Longer Journey. *Album*/Anderson, op. cit., p. 20.

64. Fate of Every Truth. *Civilization*/Naish, op. cit., p. 255.

65. Let Us Work. *Animal*/Joy, op. cit., p. 179. From *Atlantis.*

65. For All Creation. *Animal*/Joy, op. cit., p. 188. From *Journal.*

Inside back cover. *Anthology*/Joy, op. cit., p. 315. From *Revue des Travaux de l'Academie des Sciences Morales et Politiques.* Paris. 1952.

Back cover. *Life,* op. cit., p. 157.

Photographs © Erica Anderson, Albert Schweitzer Center, or courtesy of that collection, unless noted as follows:

P. 4—Fish and Wildlife Service, Department of the Interior. **P. 5**—Humane Society of the United States (HSUS)/Francesconi. **P. 8**—National Oceanic and Atmospheric Administration, Department of Commerce. **P. 15**—National Zoological Park, Smithsonian Institution. **P. 16**—HSUS. **P. 22**—Eliot Elisofon, National Museum of African Art, Eliot Elisofon Archives, Smithsonian Institution. **P. 29**—V.A. Livingstone. **P. 32**—U.S. Army Military Institute, Carlisle Barracks, Pa. **P. 33**—HSUS/Franz Dantzler. **P. 34**—Defenders of Wildlife/Interior. **P. 35**—Department of the Interior. **P. 38**—Ann Cottrell Free. **P. 39**—HSUS/Cindy Rossa. **P. 40**—HSUS. **P. 49**—Charles R. Joy. **P. 52**—Ann Cottrell Free. **P. 54**—U.S. Air Force. **P. 55**—HSUS/John Dommers. **PP. 56 & 57**—The Animal Welfare Institute. **P. 61**—National Aeronautics and Space Administration. **P. 61**—Rachel Carson Council/Erich Hartmann. **Front and End Papers**—Eliot Elisofon, National Museum of African Art, Eliot Elisofon Archives, Smithsonian Institution.

BIBLIOGRAPHY

The following books have been valuable in the production of *Animals, Nature and Albert Schweitzer*. An asterisk denotes those from which selections have been reprinted by kind permission of their publishers or copyright holders.

BOOKS BY ALBERT SCHWEITZER

African Notebook. Translated from *Afrikanische Geschichten* by Mrs. C.E.B. Russell. New York: Henry Holt and Co. 1939.

* *Indian Thought and Its Development.* Translated from *Die Weltanschauung der indischen Denker* by Mrs. C.E.B. Russell. New York: Henry Holt and Co. 1938.

* *Memoirs of Childhood and Youth.* Translated from *Aus Meiner Kindheit und Jugendzeit* by C.T. Campion. New York: The Macmillan Co. 1949.

* *On the Edge of the Primeval Forest and More from the Primeval Forest.* Translated from *Zwishen Wasser und Urwald und Das Spittal im Urwald* by C.T. Campion. New York: The Macmillan Co. 1956.

* *Out of My Life and Thought.* Translated from *Aus Meinen leben und Denkin* by C.T. Campion. New York: Henry Holt and Co. 1949.

* The *Philosophy of Civilization (Kulturphilosophie)* Part I, *Decay and Restoration of Civilization (Verfall und Weideraufbau)* and Part II, *Civilization and Ethics (Kultur und Ethik)* both translated by C.T. Campion. London: A & C Black, 1946, 1949; New York: The Macmillan Co., 1949; paperback reprint edition, Macmillan 1949 by permission of Rhena Schweitzer Miller, Tallahassee: University Presses of Florida, 1981. Part II, *Civilization and Ethics*, translated by John Naish. London: A & C Black, 1923.

* *Peace or Atomic War?* (Three broadcasts from Oslo.) New York: Holt, Rinehart and Winston. 1958.

* *The Problem of Peace in the World Today* (Nobel Peace Prize address). New York: Harper and Row. 1954.

* *Reverence for Life.* Sermons of Albert Schweitzer. Translated by Reginald Fuller. New York: Harper and Row. 1969.

* *The Teaching of Reverence for Life.* Translated by Richard and Clare Winston. New York: Holt, Rinehart and Winston. 1965.

SCHWEITZER ANTHOLOGIES

* *Albert Schweitzer: An Anthology.* Edited by Charles R. Joy. Boston: Beacon Press. 1947.

* *Albert Schweitzer: Thoughts for Our Times.* Edited by Erica Anderson. Mount Vernon, N.Y.: Peter Pauper Press. 1975.

* *The Animal World of Albert Schweitzer.* Edited and translated by Charles R. Joy. Boston: Beacon Press. 1950.

BOOKS ABOUT ALBERT SCHWEITZER

* Anderson, Erica. *The Schweitzer Album.* New York: Harper and Row. 1965.

Brabazon, James. *Albert Schweitzer.* New York: G.P. Putnam's Sons. 1975.

Cousins, Norman (with Clara Urquhart). *Dr. Schweitzer of Lambaréné.* New York: Harper and Brothers. 1960.

Ice, Jackson Lee. *Prophet of Radical Theology.* Philadelphia: The Westminster Press. 1971.

Marshall, George and Poling, David. *Schweitzer: A Biography.* New York: Doubleday and Co. 1975.

Ratter, Magnus. *Albert Schweitzer: Life and Message.* Boston: Beacon Press. 1950.

Seaver, George. *Albert Schweitzer, the Man and His Mind.* New York: Harper and Brothers. 1947.

SCHWEITZER PERIODICALS IN U.S.A.

* *The Courier,* New York: Albert Schweitzer Fellowship.

Reverence, Great Barrington: Albert Schweitzer Center.

GUIDES TO MAJOR ALBERT SCHWEITZER MATERIAL

Albert Schweitzer, an International Bibliography. Compiled and edited by Laura Person, Nancy Griffith, Antje B. Lemke. Boston: G.K. Hall, 70 Lincoln St. (02135) 1982.

Guide to Albert Schweitzer Collections in the United States. Compiled and edited by Haidee Flinders and Antje B. Lemke. New York: Albert Schweitzer Fellowship, 866 United Nations Plaza (10017) 1981.

In Europe: Albert Schweitzer Central Archives, Maison Albert Schweitzer, F 68140 Gunsbach, Haut-Rhin, France.

ACKNOWLEDGEMENTS

The cooperation and assistance extended by individuals and organizations, dedicated to the Schweitzer ethic, has been heartening. To each of them, my appreciation for their interest in the creation of this small volume. This second edition, published by the Flying Fox Press, includes several additions and revisions, designed to heighten understanding and knowledge of Albert Schweitzer and his philosophy.

Some of the new material, obtained since the first edition in 1982, can be found on pages 4, 26, 61 and documented in "sources for selection" section. I am grateful to Schweitzer scholar, Dr. Antje Lemke, for her discovery of the long-standing mistranslation or misprinting of the always puzzling intent of the young Schweitzer to shoot birds (page 4) due to peer pressure when in truth, his was the opposite intent.

Among those persons to whom I extend particular gratitude are Charles F. Herrmann III, Rhena Schweitzer Miller, Dr. Lemke, Estelle Linzer, Christine Stevens. Jessie Despard, Dr. Kathleen Collins, Edouard Nies-Berger, Toni van Leer, James Sinclair, John Dommers, Dorothy and Lee Ellerbrock, Dr. John F. Kullberg, Bella Chaikin, Virginia Warren, Dr. Michael W. Fox, Margaret Marciante, Harriet and Morris Cobern, my husband, James Stillman Free, our daughter, Elissa Blake Free and her husband, William Ward Nooter. The cooperation of the Albert Schweitzer Fellowship and the Albert Schweitzer Center has been most valuable.

The helpful suggestions of the late Ali Silver, who so well served Dr. Schweitzer and his memory — both in Lambaréné and Gunsbach — were not forgotten.

I am grateful to the publishers of the English translations of Dr. Schweitzer's works who granted permission to quote from those editions. My appreciation, also, to the Albert Schweitzer Center for the courtesy of permitting use of photographs by the Center's founder, Erica Anderson.

And to the readers, my profound gratitude, for without you, Albert Schweitzer's message of "reverence for life" would be even more difficult to spread.

Ann Cottrell Free
Washington, D.C.

THE FLYING FOX PRESS
4204 Forty-Fifth Street, N.W.
Washington, D.C. 20016
(301) 229-8160
(202) 537-1434
— Established 1987 —

Publisher: *No Room, Save In The Heart*
Poetry and Prose On Reverence for Life —
Animals, Nature & Humankind
by Ann Cottrell Free

The flying fox (Pteropas poliocephalus) is a vegetarian fruit bat commonly found in the Southeastern hemisphere. In 1986 Dr. John D. Pettigrew, University of Queensland, Australia, postulated with some certainty that this flying mammal, unlike other bats, may be a member of the primate family, hence the only flying primate—man or ape.

Cover Design by Mary L. Kaido

80

Ann Cottrell Free is an author, poet, journalist, 1963 Albert Schweitzer Medalist and 1987 recipient of the Rachel Carson Legacy Award.

Charles F. Herrmann III, a former editor at the Humane Society of the United States, is a member of the editorial staff, the National Geographic Society.

Erica Anderson, founder of the Albert Schweitzer Center, was a photographer, author and journalist, who spent many years at the Schweitzer Hospital in Lambaréné, Gabon.